Saint Patrick's Day

BY ANN HEINRICHS • ILLUSTRATED BY JOEL SNYDER

The Child's World

Published by The Child's World®
1980 Lookout Drive • Mankato, MN 56003-1705
800-599-READ • www.childsworld.com

Acknowledgments
The Child's World®: Mary Berendes, Publishing Director
The Design Lab: Design
Jody Jensen Shaffer: Editing

ISBN 9781623235123
LCCN 2013931386

Printed in the United States of America
Mankato, MN
March, 2014
PA02227

ABOUT THE AUTHOR

Ann Heinrichs lives in Chicago, Illinois. She has written more than two hundred books for children. She loves traveling to faraway places.

ABOUT THE ILLUSTRATOR

Joel Snyder is a graduate of the Rhode Island School of Design. He lives in New York with his son, a beagle, and twelve tropical fish.

Table of Contents

CHAPTER 1

Happy Saint Patrick's Day!

Bands are marching down the street. The sound of bagpipes fills the air. And everyone is wearing green. It's Saint Patrick's Day!

Saint Patrick's Day is a joyful holiday. It's a time to celebrate being Irish. But you don't have to be Irish to join in. People like to say, "Everyone's Irish on Saint Patrick's Day!"

Would you like to learn a Saint Patrick's Day greeting? Just say, *"Erin go bragh* (EHR-in go BRAH)!" It means "Ireland forever!"

Listen to the bagpipes! It must be Saint Patrick's Day.

*Patrick was kidnapped and sold
into slavery in Ireland. Once there,
he worked as a shepherd.*

CHAPTER 2

Who Was Saint Patrick?

Saint Patrick is the **patron saint** of Ireland. He lived more than 1,500 years ago. Patrick was born in Great Britain. When he was sixteen, outlaws kidnapped him. They sold him as a slave in Ireland. There he tended sheep for his master.

While a slave, Patrick's faith grew stronger. One day, he escaped. Then he became a Christian missionary. Patrick traveled through much of Ireland. He spread his faith wherever he went.

Many Irish people believed in several gods then. But Patrick taught about the one God. He was often in danger for his teachings. But he bravely kept on. The Irish people loved him for his kindness. And they still love him today!

Saint Patrick's Day is March 17. That's believed to be the date of Patrick's death.

Ireland is an island. Beautiful green grass covers the hillsides. That's why Ireland is called the **Emerald** Isle.

Patrick preached Christianity throughout Ireland.

An Irish Blessing

May there always be work
     for your hands to do,
May your purse always hold
     a coin or two.
May the sun always shine
warm on your windowpane,
May a rainbow be certain to
     follow each rain.
May the hand of a friend
     always be near you,
And may God fill your heart
with gladness to cheer you.

—Author unknown

*According to popular legend,
Saint Patrick drove the snakes
out of Ireland.*

CHAPTER 3

The Legend of the Snakes

Many legends, or tales, were created about Saint
Patrick. One legend says that snakes covered the
land. Saint Patrick stood high on a hill. With his
wooden staff, he drove the snakes into the sea. At
last, Ireland was safe.

This story probably has a hidden meaning. The
snakes stand for Ireland's old religions. Saint Patrick
drove them out with Christianity.

CHAPTER 4

Saint Patrick and the Shamrock

The shamrock is the national plant of Ireland.

Saint Patrick used the shamrock as a symbol for the Trinity.

Another legend tells about the shamrock. That's a three-leaf clover. Saint Patrick used it to explain the Trinity—the Father, Son, and Holy Spirit. All three, he said, are God. Yet there is only one God.

In the same way, shamrocks have three leaves. But they grow on just one stem. People welcomed this lesson. Now people wear shamrocks on Saint Patrick's Day. The shamrock is still an important **symbol** of Ireland.

Saint Patrick's Green

Oh, I love to see
  the shamrocks
Boys wear March seventeen,
And I love the girls'
  green ribbons,
And bits of evergreen;
For they stand for brave
  Saint Patrick,
So fearless and so good—
Oh! The Irish ought
  to love him,
Just as everybody should!

—*Bertha E. Bush*

Saint Patrick's Day parades have long been a holiday tradition in U.S. cities.

CHAPTER 5

A Grand Holiday

Many Irish people came to the American **colonies**. They brought their customs to their new home. One was celebrating Saint Patrick's Day!

This holiday began as a religious feast. But it quickly became a big public event. Boston, Massachusetts, celebrated Saint Patrick's Day in 1737. New York City held a parade in 1762. Soon other cities joined in.

The parades were grand affairs. Irish clubs provided marching bands. Firefighters and police officers joined in, too. So did the mayor and other leaders. It was a great day for the Irish!

CHAPTER 6

Symbols and Decorations

Shamrocks are everywhere on Saint Patrick's Day. You'll see four-leaf clovers, too. They're signs of good luck. People often speak of the "luck of the Irish."

Leprechauns (LEP-ruh-kahnz) are favorite decorations. These magical little men hide in the forest. What if you catch a leprechaun? He must lead you to his pot of gold! It's hidden at the end of a rainbow.

Shillelaghs (shuh-LAY-leez) are Irish symbols, too. These sturdy sticks were once used for protection.

The Leprechaun's Gold

A leprechaun is
   small and green—
He hides where he
   cannot be seen.
But if you catch one
   on this day,
He must give his gold away!

—*Author unknown*

Leprechauns are a famous symbol for Saint Patrick's Day.

The harp is another Irish symbol. It's sometimes called the Brian Boru harp. Brian Boru was an Irish king. He lived about one thousand years ago. He brought the Irish nation together.

CHAPTER 7

How We Celebrate

You'd better wear green on Saint Patrick's Day. If you don't, people can pinch you! You'll see green everywhere that day. It stands for Ireland, the Emerald Isle.

Ouch! Wear green on Saint Patrick's Day to avoid getting pinched.

Saint Patrick's Day parades are noisy! Floats and marching bands go by. Some bands play bagpipes. The musicians are wearing **kilts**. Other bands play loud brass horns. And booming drums keep a marching beat.

The crowds are a sea of green. People are wearing green hats and clothes. They're shouting "Erin go bragh!" Everyone is Irish today!

Corned beef and cabbage are **traditional** holiday foods. So are Irish stew and soda bread. They make a hearty meal after the parade.

Saint Patrick's Day

Leprechauns peeking
Around a willow tree,
Pussy willows waking,
Longing to be free.
Colleens and shamrocks
And castles old and gray,
Put them all together
To make Saint Patrick's Day!

—Author unknown

CHAPTER 8

Saint Patrick's Day around the World

Irish people live all over the world. They love to celebrate Saint Patrick's Day. Even some cities in Asia celebrate.

Ireland is a festive place that day. Many people wear a little bunch of shamrocks. Dublin, Ireland's capital, holds the Saint Patrick's Festival. It lasts a whole week! There are parades, music, and fireworks.

New York City's parade is the largest in the world. More than 150,000 people take part. Chicago, Illinois, has a big parade, too. The city dyes the Chicago River green!

Saint Patrick's Day Poem

Saint Patrick came
from Ireland,
A country trimmed
with green.
It has the shamrocks
and the pipes—
Those leprechauns
you've seen.
Those leprechauns
will trip you—
You'll fall flat on your face.
They'll tickle your nose
and sour the milk,
Then find a hiding place!

—Author unknown

Saint Patrick's Day is popular all over the world.

Saint Patrick's Day

CHAPTER 9

Poetry Corner

I'LL WEAR A SHAMROCK

Saint Patrick's Day is with us,
The day when all that's seen
To right and left and everywhere
Is green, green, green!
And Irish tunes they whistle
And Irish songs they sing,
Today each Irish lad walks out
As proud as any king.
I'll wear a four-leaf shamrock
In my coat, the glad day through,
For my father and mother are Irish
And I am Irish, too!

—*Mary Carolyn Davies (1888–1966)*

LEPRECHAUN, LEPRECHAUN

Leprechaun, leprechaun, fly across the sea

And fetch an emerald shamrock for you and me.

Do not bring a nettle or a thistle for a joke,

But bring an Irish shamrock, for we are Irish folk.

And you and I, my leprechaun, will wear the shamrock gay,

And match it with an Irish smile upon Saint Patrick's Day!

—*Author unknown*

I'M LOOKING OVER A FOUR-LEAF CLOVER

I'm looking over a four-leaf clover

That I overlooked before.

One leaf is sunshine, the second is rain,

Third is the roses that grow in the lane.

No need explaining, the one remaining

Is somebody I adore.

I'm looking over a four-leaf clover

That I overlooked before.

—Song; words by Mort Dixon (1892–1956)

Joining in the Spirit of Saint Patrick's Day

* Look at a map of the world. Can you find Ireland? Is it larger or smaller than your state?

* Do you know someone with an Irish background? Ask about his or her family history.

* Write an Irish blessing. It should be full of good wishes. Begin each line with "May you…" or "May your…."

* Does your city have a Saint Patrick's Day parade? Go and enjoy the fun!

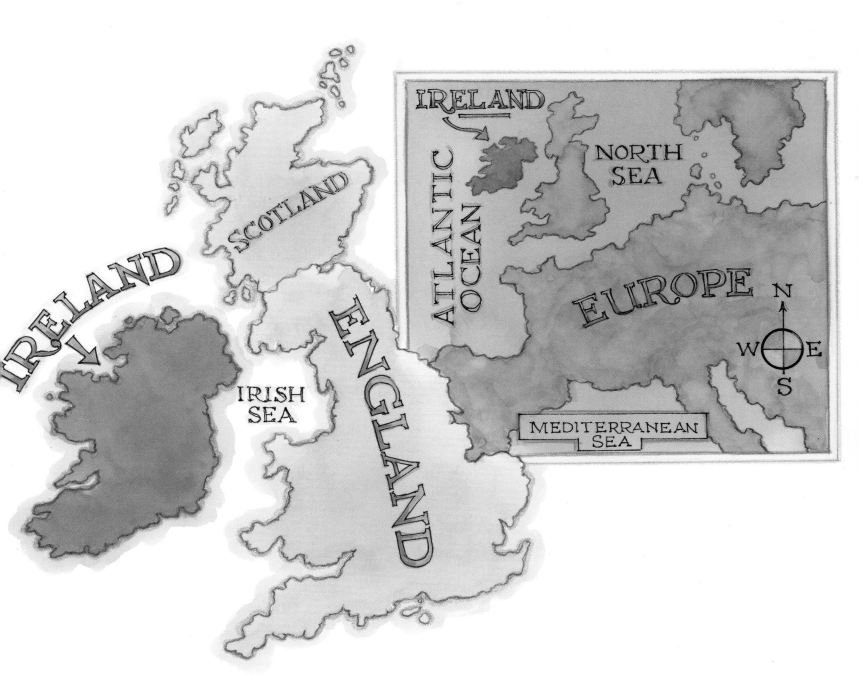

IRELAND

SCOTLAND

IRELAND

IRISH
SEA

ENGLAND

IRELAND

ATLANTIC
OCEAN

NORTH
SEA

EUROPE

MEDITERRANEAN
SEA

N
W   E
S

Making Irish Soda Bread

What you need:

2 cups all-purpose flour

1 cup whole wheat flour

2 teaspoons baking powder

$^1/_2$ teaspoon salt

$^1/_2$ cup sugar

2 eggs

$1\,^1/_2$ cups buttermilk or plain yogurt

$^3/_4$ cup raisins

Cooking spray or a stick of butter/margarine

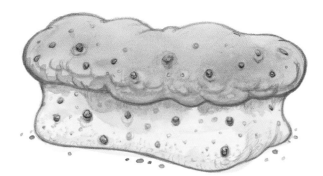

Directions

1. Preheat the oven to 350 degrees Fahrenheit.[*]
2. Place the baking powder, salt, sugar, and both kinds of flour in a bowl.
3. Stir in the eggs and buttermilk (or yogurt).
4. Add the raisins and stir again.
5. Next, sprinkle a little flour onto a baking board or some other clean, flat surface. Pour your doughy mixture onto this surface and knead ten times.
6. Use your hands to shape the dough into a loaf.
7. Finally, grease a loaf pan with cooking spray or a small amount of butter (or margarine).
8. Place the loaf in the pan and cook for one hour.
9. Allow the bread to cool before removing it from the pan. When it's ready, your tasty treat should feed about twelve people—and maybe a few leprechauns!

[*]*Have an adult help you operate the oven.*

Making a Pot o' Gold

Those tricky leprechauns never let you get near their pots of gold, so how about making your own?

What you need:

A paper plate

A cardboard tube
   (empty toilet-paper roll or paper-towel roll)

Glue

Paint or markers

Gold glitter

Scissors

Directions

1. Cut down the toilet-paper roll or paper-towel roll so it is about 2 inches high.
2. Paint or color it black.
3. Cut the paper plate in half.
4. Cut out a rainbow shape from the outside edge of one half of the plate. Make sure the end of the rainbow shape will fit inside the painted cardboard tube.
5. Paint or color the rainbow-shaped cutout so that it has all the colors of a rainbow.
6. When the paint or marker ink is dry, put one end of your rainbow inside the black cardboard tube. Glue it in place.
7. Put some glue on the top edge of the cardboard tube and sprinkle gold glitter on top of the glue. Let the glue dry.

Now you have your very own pot of gold at the end of a rainbow.

Glossary

colleens—Irish girls

colonies—lands with ties to another country

emerald—a green jewel

kilts—pleated skirts sometimes worn by Irish and Scottish men

patron saint—a holy person special to a group of people

symbol—an object that stands for an idea

traditional—following old customs

Learn More

Books

DePaola , Tomie. *Patrick: Patron Saint of Ireland*. New York: Holiday House, 1992.

Gnojewski, Carol. *St. Patrick's Day Crafts*. Berkeley Heights, NJ: Enslow Publishers, 2004.

Krull, Kathleen, and David McPhail (illustrator.) *A Pot o' Gold: A Treasury of Irish Stories, Poetry, Folklore, and (of Course) Blarney*. New York: Hyperion Books for Children, 2004.

Nolan, Janet, and Ben F. Stahl (illustrator). *The St. Patrick's Day Shillelagh*. Morton Grove, IL: Albert Whitman & Company, 2002.

Web Sites

Visit our Web site for links about Saint Patrick's Day and other holidays:

childsworld.com/links

Note to Parents, Teachers, and Librarians: We routinely verify our Web links to make sure they are safe and active sites. So encourage your readers to check them out!

Index